SAN FRANCISCO

A good place for a city? Perhaps not. The weather changes quickly, and often cold white fog comes in over the bridge. There are about seventy hills (forty-three of them with names), and some of them are very steep. There is water on three sides of the city; the views are good, but getting in and out of the city is not always easy. And earthquakes bring fire, and sometimes death . . .

But millions of people come to San Francisco every year. They come to walk around the city and ride on the cable cars. They visit the neighbourhood of the hippies, and eat wonderful food from the sea. San Francisco is not the same as other cities – and that is why they love it.

OXFORD BOOKWORMS LIBRARY
Factfiles

San Francisco
Stage 1 (400 headwords)

Factfiles Series Editor: Christine Lindop

The author would like to thank San Franciscans Wanda Nichols and Jill Shutz for all their help.

JANET HARDY-GOULD

San Francisco

OXFORD UNIVERSITY PRESS

OXFORD
UNIVERSITY PRESS

Great Clarendon Street, Oxford, OX2 6DP, United Kingdom

Oxford University Press is a department of the University of Oxford.
It furthers the University's objective of excellence in research, scholarship,
and education by publishing worldwide. Oxford is a registered trade
mark of Oxford University Press in the UK and in certain other countries

The moral rights of the author have been asserted

First published 2012

10 9 8 7 6 5

ISBN: 978 0 19 479437 4

A complete recording of *San Francisco* is available

Printed in China

Word count (main text): 5,664

For more information on the Oxford Bookworms Library,
visit www.oup.com/elt/bookworms

ACKNOWLEDGEMENTS

Maps: pp.3, 17 Peter Bull

The publishers would like to thank the following for their permission to reproduce photographs: Alamy
Images pp.4 (Colorful mural/Nitish Naharas), 5 (Fog over San Francisco/Brad Perks Lightscapes),
6 (Bullitt film poster/Moviestore Collection Ltd.), 6 (Vertigo film poster/AF archive), 9 (Gold
nuggets/Sergey Goruppa), 11 (Wells Fargo stagecoach/Martin Thomas Photography), 15 (San
Francisco, 1967/Pictorial Press Ltd), 22 (Cable car/Richard Wareham Fotografie), 23 (Golden
Gate Bridge at dusk/JLImages), 25 (Golden Gate Bridge/Bob Kreisel), 30 (Rollerblading/Lonely
Planet Images), 31 (San Francisco Cable Car Museum/Mark Morgan), 34 (Chinese New Year
celebrations/Judy Bellah), 35 (San Francisco Giants game/Ron Niebrugge), 38 (Clam chowder in
sourdough bread bowl/Karin Lau), 39 (Recycling bins/Green Stock Media); Corbis pp.1 (Chinese
railroad workers/Bettmann), 10 (Panning for gold/Bettmann), 10 (California and the Gold Region
Direct! Poster/Bettmann), 12 (Ruins after earthquake), 14 (Lighted Grounds at Panama Pacific
Exposition/Schenectady Museum; Hall of Electrical History Foundation), 18 (Transamerica
Pyramid/Rudy Sulgan), 19 (Lombard Street/Ron Watts), 20 (Steiner Street, San Francisco/Clive
Sawyer PCL/SuperStock), 22 (Poet Maya Angelou/Bettmann), 26 (Alcatraz Island/Cameron
Davidson), 26 (Al Capone/Bettmann), 27 (Alcatraz cell/Terry W.Eggers), 29 (Bridge in Japanese
Team Garden/Myopia), 30 (Buffalo in Golden Gate park/Kevin Fleming), 32 (Old Wells Fargo
wooden box/Ed Young), 33 (California Academy of Sciences Building/Art on File), 36 (Neiman
Marcus skylight/Morton Beebe), 37 (City Lights bookstore/Morton Beebe), 40 (Man with bike/
Woods Wheatcroft/Aurora Photos),; fotolibra.com pp.8 (San Francisco Mission/John Lander),
13 (Lotta's Fountain/Sergio Lanza); Getty Images pp.0 (San Francisco cable car/Mitchell Funk),
7 (Spanish explorers spy San Francisco Bay/National Geographic); Oxford University Press
pp.44 (Sandy beach/Photodisc), 44 (St James Park/Comstock), 44 (Grand Teto National Park/
Photodisc), 44 (Bus/Images USA), 44 (Bush fire/Imagebroker), 44 (Rio de Janeiro/Image Broker).

CONTENTS

1   The city of hills

Every year, about sixteen million visitors come to San Francisco on the west coast of the United States. Most people arrive in this wonderful city in California by car, bus, or plane. But some take the train and go across the country on the famous old railroad.

You can get on a train in New York on the east coast and travel to the city of Chicago. From there, you can make one of the world's most exciting train journeys – from the window, you can see fast rivers, red mountains, big green trees, and many wild animals.

At first, you go past the towns and villages of Iowa and Nebraska, next through the big Rocky Mountains, then across the open country of Utah, and in the end through the mountains of the famous Sierra Nevada. Three days after you leave New York, you arrive in the city of San Francisco – a wonderful finish to a beautiful journey!

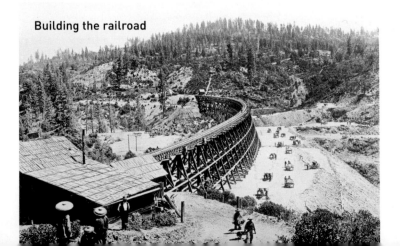

Building the railroad

This railroad across the United States first opened in 1869. It carried thousands of people to San Francisco, and the city became bigger every year. Men and women began to call this exciting place 'The Paris of the West'. These early visitors travelled to San Francisco because they wanted to make money and have a new life. But why do millions of people come to this city today?

Many visitors are interested in the famous places there – they want to walk across the wonderful Golden Gate Bridge, sit in the beautiful Golden Gate Park or visit the island prison of Alcatraz.

But they also want to see the nice views. San Francisco is nearly an island – it has water on three sides. There is the Pacific Ocean on the west side, San Francisco Bay on the east side and the Golden Gate with its famous bridge on the north side. The city is smaller than other American cities – it only has 800,000 people. But many people live in towns like Oakland, thirteen kilometres away, and come to work in San Francisco every day.

There are about seventy hills in San Francisco, so it is a very good place for photographers. You can stand on a hill and take wonderful pictures of San Francisco with the blue water behind it. But you need to be very quick with your camera because the weather often changes here. One minute you can see big blue skies, and the next minute there is only the famous white fog – this moves quickly across the city from the sea.

A lot of visitors love San Francisco because it does not feel like a big city. The hills break the town into different parts – these are called neighbourhoods.

N

Sausalito

San
Francisco
Bay

Golden
Gate Bridge

Oakland

Pacific
Ocean

San
Francisco

Golden Gate Park

San
Francisco
Bay

Alcatraz

Golden
Gate
Bridge

FISHERMAN'S
WHARF

TELEGRAPH
HILL

RUSSIAN
HILL

NORTH
BEACH

PACIFIC
HEIGHTS

NOB
HILL

CHINA
TOWN

JAPANTOWN

Market Street

Alamo
Square

Golden
Gate
Park

HAIGHT
ASHBURY

Mission
Dolores

CASTRO

MISSION

Every neighbourhood has its coffee shops, restaurants, and little supermarkets. Forty-three of the hills have names, and some of the neighbourhoods take their names from them. For example, in the downtown part in the east of the city there is Nob Hill, Russian Hill, and Telegraph Hill.

Over the years, many families from across the world moved to the city. Today, some of these neighbourhoods have a lot of people and shops from one country. For example, there is the famous Chinatown with its wonderful Chinese restaurants or the newer Japantown with its Japanese food shops and bookshops.

Many men and women come to the city because it is an open, free place too. In neighbourhoods like the Mission, many people like to meet and talk about new ideas. When you sit in one of the coffee shops there, you sometimes hear people talk interestingly about new and different things.

Colour on the streets

The bridge in the fog

Last of all, visitors come because they learn about the city from hundreds of films and books. For example, the writer Jack London was born in San Francisco in 1876. He was from a family of workers, but he later became famous for his exciting books *The Call of the Wild* and *White Fang*. In some of his stories, like *Martin Eden*, you can learn about the lives of people in old San Francisco.

The writer Dashiell Hammett lived in the city in the 1920s. He wrote wonderful detective stories – often with the famous San Francisco fog in them. Perhaps the best of these is *The Maltese Falcon*. It became an important Hollywood film in 1941 with Humphrey Bogart.

Some later books were very different from these earlier stories. For example, *The Joy Luck Club* by Amy Tan is about four families in the Chinatown neighbourhood. It looks at the lives of older Chinese women and their Chinese-American daughters.

Of course, many visitors remember the films too. Who can forget *Vertigo* by Alfred Hitchcock? In this 1958 film, a San Francisco detective is watching a young woman and she suddenly jumps from under the Golden Gate Bridge into the cold water. The detective does not like tall buildings or bridges but he quickly jumps down and helps her.

Many books and films use the San Francisco fog, but one film famously uses the big hills of the city. This was the 1968 film *Bullitt* with Steve McQueen. It has a very long car chase up and down the hills – it is one of the most exciting car chases in the world of film!

When you say the words 'San Francisco', something interesting often happens. People begin to sing! They sing something called 'I Left My Heart in San Francisco'. The singer Tony Bennett first sang this in the famous Fairmont Hotel in the city in the 1960s.

Most visitors know a lot of stories about San Francisco today from the cinema, TV, and radio. But how much do they know about the early days of the city?

2   Early days

People began to live in the San Francisco area thousands of years ago. They were Native Americans, and in this part of the country they were called the Ohlone. They lived in villages along the coast and found things to eat in the rivers or the sea. This seafood and the wild animals were an important part of their usual food.

But the lives of the Ohlone changed suddenly in the late 1700s when early travellers from Europe came to the area. A Spanish soldier called Captain Juan Bautista de Anza arrived on the coast and he made a building at the Golden Gate in 1776. Then the Spanish opened a mission here – the Mission San Francisco de Asís. The city of San Francisco later took its name from this place.

The Spanish arrive near San Francisco

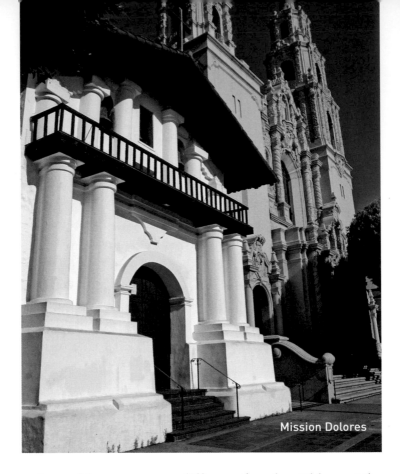
Mission Dolores

Everything was now different for the Ohlone. The Spanish needed workers, and they took many of the Ohlone to live in the mission. The Spanish brought new diseases with them too, and about three-quarters of the Ohlone people became ill from these and died.

There were a number of different mission buildings, but the last one was built in 1791. You can visit this beautiful place today. It is now called Mission Dolores and it is the oldest building in San Francisco.

In 1821, the area stopped being Spanish and became part of the country of Mexico. People built houses away from the mission and they began a little town called Yerba Buena.

Between 1846 and 1848, there was a war between the United States and Mexico. On 2 February 1848, California became part of the United States and the town soon changed its name from Yerba Buena to San Francisco.

Before this time, there were not many people in the town or the area around it. But things changed one day in January 1848. At Sutter's Mill, a place 190 kilometres to the north-east of San Francisco, a worker called James Marshall found something interesting in a river. He worked for a man called John Sutter, so he quickly went to him and told him about it. What did Marshall find? Soon the two men knew the answer – it was gold!

John Sutter did not want to tell people about the gold. But one important man soon heard about it – this was Samuel Brannan of the newspaper the *California Star*. He walked quickly through the streets of San Francisco with some gold in a bottle in his hand and said, 'Gold! Gold! Gold on the American River!'

Of course, the people of the town all left at once and went to look for the gold. So San Francisco became very quiet, with nobody on the streets. But then newspapers around the world wrote about the story. They talked about 'mountains of gold' in California and the famous Californian 'gold rush' began!

Pieces of gold

CALIFORNIA AND THE GOLD REGION DIRECT!

The Magnificent, Fast Sailing and favorite packet Ship,

JOSEPHINE,

BURTHEN 400 TONS, CAPT.

10th November Next.

RODNEY FRENCH, No. 103 North Water Street, Rodman's Wharf.

Looking for gold

In the gold rush people came in their thousands to California. They all wanted the same thing – to find gold, and to find it quickly. Around 40,000 people came across the United States, often on foot. Thousands of travellers arrived by ship from Europe, China, and Australia too. They were called the Forty-niners – because many of them came to California in 1849.

A lot of these visitors stayed in San Francisco before and after their journey north to the gold areas. The number of people in the town suddenly went from 1,000 in 1848 to 25,000 in 1850! Hundreds of new hotels, restaurants, and places to drink opened and the town soon became a wild place.

Some travellers in the early days found gold easily and made lots of money. But many people soon lost it in the streets of San Francisco. The hotels and restaurants often made more money than the Forty-niners!

The Californian gold rush finished in 1855. Some people went home, but many stayed and opened businesses. San Francisco changed from a little town into a city.

Some of the most famous San Francisco businesses come from this time. For example, the Wells Fargo bank and stagecoach business opened in 1852. The Wells Fargo stagecoaches brought letters and travellers from across the United States to California. The roads were very bad and dangerous but the stagecoaches usually arrived on time!

The stagecoaches and the new railroad across the United States opened San Francisco to people from across the country, and big ships from around the world often stopped here too.

In the late 1800s, many rich people began to build beautiful houses in neighbourhoods like Nob Hill. But the city later lost many of these on one very bad day in the spring of 1906.

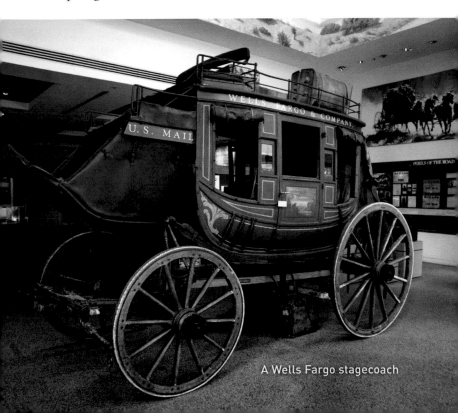

A Wells Fargo stagecoach

3 From 1906 to the Summer of Love

At 5.12 in the morning on Wednesday 18 April 1906, the earth suddenly began to move in San Francisco. Most people were at home in bed. All over the city, men, women, and children sat up when they heard a long and terrible noise. The earth did not stop moving for forty-two seconds. It was a very big earthquake – one of the worst earthquakes in the world at that time.

Families ran out of their homes and saw a different city. Most of the houses, shops, and hotels were not there any longer. Soon, fires began in different neighbourhoods and they moved quickly from place to place.

After the earthquake

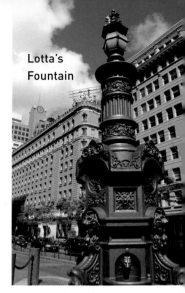
Lotta's
Fountain

People wanted to stop the fires but there was not a lot of water – only one fountain called Lotta's Fountain. Soldiers and other workers stood in a long line and took water from the fountain. The water went from one person to the next, but it was slow work. The fires only stopped after four long days.

More than three thousand men, women, and children died in the earthquake or the terrible fires, and more than half of the people lost their homes. Many began to sleep in open places like the Golden Gate Park.

Countries around the world quickly learned about the disaster. For the first time, newspaper readers saw pictures of a city after an earthquake. Countries like the United Kingdom and Canada, and rich business people in the United States, gave money to the city.

Very soon, all the builders began to build new houses, restaurants, and shops – fifteen every day! In the years after the earthquake, San Francisco became a wonderful city again, ready for a big exhibition in 1915. This was called the Panama-Pacific International Exposition. Thousands of people came here from all over the United States. They could see exciting new things and eat different food from countries around the Pacific.

In the 1920s and 1930s, San Francisco became more important. Hundreds of ships from around the world came and went every week. In the Second World War big ships were built there too.

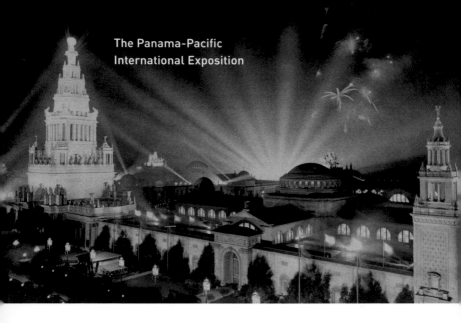

The Panama-Pacific International Exposition

After the war, writers and thinkers with interesting new ideas came to San Francisco. In the 1950s they moved into neighbourhoods like North Beach and Haight Ashbury. The most famous of these people was Jack Kerouac. Many young students read his 1957 book *On the Road*. In the book he travels around the United States and goes to San Francisco a number of times.

Perhaps one of the most exciting years was 1967. Over 100,000 young people travelled to San Francisco. Most of them were hippies with big hats, long clothes, and flowers in their hair. These hippies stayed in the Haight Ashbury neighbourhood and they ate, sang, and talked about ideas – all in one place. This time was called the 'Summer of Love' and people around the world saw it on TV.

From the time of the 1960s and 1970s, the city became famous for its open ideas. San Francisco was a good place for people from different countries and with different lives. Many visitors loved the place so they stayed and opened shops or coffee shops in some of the more exciting young neighbourhoods.

Of course, this was only one part of life in San Francisco. The city became important in the world of banks and businesses too. In the 1990s, a lot of new internet businesses quickly opened with money from the banks. In March 2000, many of these businesses suddenly closed again, after the banks wanted their money back. But today the city is famous again for its banks and new businesses.

A hippy from the Summer of Love

4   The fog and the fault

The weather in San Francisco is often different from other American cities because it is very near the water, between the Pacific Ocean and San Francisco Bay. The waters of the sea are very important to the temperature in the city – the weather here is never very hot or very cold. The temperature in the winter does not change a lot from the temperature in the summer. For example, in the day it is often 15 °C in February and 19 °C in August.

The people of San Francisco laugh about their famous summers. The weather is usually worse in the summer months of June, July, and August. At this time of year a lot of fog comes from the Pacific Ocean, through the Golden Gate and into the city, and you sometimes need to wear a coat – in summer! The best weather is often in the spring in April and May or in the autumn in September and October when it is nice and warm with not much rain.

The weather can be very different from one neighbourhood to the next. You can sit in the hot sun in one area, then walk for five minutes to a different place and suddenly there is fog or rain!

The Pacific Ocean changes the daily weather in San Francisco. But there is one other important thing in the life of the city – the San Andreas Fault. This is a big line between two parts of the earth, and when one part hits the other this can make big earthquakes.

The San Andreas Fault does not go through San Francisco but it goes near the city to the south. The terrible earthquake of 1906 happened because the San Andreas Fault moved. There was a very big earthquake in 1989 because of it too – it was called the Loma Prieta earthquake. More than three thousand people lost their homes and about sixty people died.

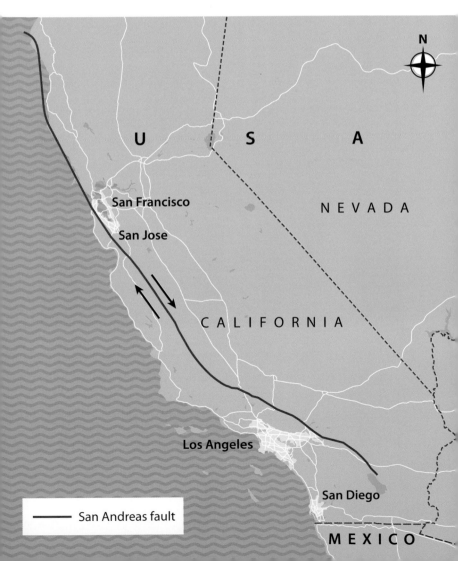

San Francisco

San Jose

NEVADA

CALIFORNIA

Los Angeles

San Diego

MEXICO

USA

N

—— San Andreas fault

There are often earthquakes today in the San Francisco area but these are very little and people cannot usually feel them. The newer houses or offices in the city are carefully built: when the earth moves, they can move too. For example, the Transamerica Pyramid, the tallest building in San Francisco, moved 30 centimetres from side to side in the 1989 earthquake but it stayed up!

5 Travel

Travel in San Francisco is often more exciting than in other places. This is because of the many hills across the city – some of these are very steep! Perhaps the most famous road on a steep hill in San Francisco is Lombard Street. Lombard Street is a long road with one very steep part on Russian Hill. In 1922, people changed the line of Lombard Street here and they made the road go from

Lombard Street

side to side down the hill. This is easier for drivers, but they need to drive from one side to the other eight times! There is no other street like this in the world, people say!

San Francisco is also different from many other American cities because it does not have any very big roads near the centre. In cities like Los Angeles or Miami, people usually drive from place to place, but in San Francisco more people go by bus or walk.

A walk in the city is always good – there are wonderful views across the hills and you can go past many nice buildings. For example, in the Haight Ashbury neighbourhood there are the beautiful old houses around Alamo Square. They are in different colours – like green, blue, orange or yellow.

Some people travel to and from the city by sea too. Workers come across the water every day from towns like

Houses in Alamo Square

Oakland or Sausalito. When they arrive they travel around on the 'Muni'. The Muni is all the bus and streetcar lines in San Francisco and the famous old cable car lines too.

Everybody knows about the cable cars – you cannot find many films about San Francisco without one! They first began in 1873. A man called Andrew Hallidie had the idea for them when he saw a bad road accident. They were a very good answer to the steep, dangerous hills and soon there were cable car lines across the city.

But San Francisco lost many of its cable cars in the terrible 1906 earthquake. After this there were more buses, and by the 1930s a lot of people used these to travel around the city. In 1947 some of the most important men in the city wanted to close the cable car lines. Of course, the people of San Francisco became very angry because they did not want to lose them.

A cable car

In the end, they saved the cable cars and today forty of the cars move around the city on three different lines. Every car has a driver, and a conductor – this man or woman takes the money and helps people when they travel too. This is important because some travellers stand out of the cable car on the side and this can be very dangerous!

One of the most famous conductors was Maya Angelou. She was the first African-American streetcar conductor in the city when she was only fourteen. She later became one of the most important writers in the United States. Her book *I Know Why the Caged Bird Sings* is about her early years and the lives of African-Americans in the 1930s.

6   The bridge and Alcatraz

When people talk about San Francisco, they often think of the long orange-red bridge to the city – the world-famous Golden Gate Bridge. There are many wonderful photos of the bridge, often with the sun behind it or the fog half over it.

A man called Charles Crocker first thought of a bridge here in 1872 but many people did not like the idea. The Golden Gate was a terrible place for a bridge, they said, because the weather was always bad and the seas were very dangerous.

Later, in 1921, a bridge builder called Joseph Strauss had a good idea for a long bridge across the Golden Gate and he talked to many important people about it. In the end they listened to him, and work began on the bridge in January 1933. It cost more than 35 million dollars and hundreds of workers built it over four years.

When it opened in April 1937, it was the longest bridge of its type in the world. It was 2.7 kilometres long and you could walk, drive, or go by bicycle across it. The first day was very exciting. Over 200,000 men, women, and children came from all over the city and walked across the new bridge.

And fifty years later in April 1987, thousands of people went across the bridge again. This time there were 300,000 walkers – some of the older men and women happily remembered their first walk across it in 1937.

Of course, this big bridge always needs a lot of work because the fog and sea water move around it all the time. You can find thirty-eight workers on the bridge every day! What do they do? They make the bridge the famous orange-red colour, and their work never stops.

You can see the Golden Gate Bridge in a lot of films too. In the James Bond film *A View to a Kill*, a dangerous man called Zorin chases Bond and they have a long fight on the bridge. They move wildly from side to side but in

Across the bridge in 1987

the end, Bond hits Zorin with his feet and he goes down into the cold waters of the Golden Gate.

When you stand on the bridge and look east across San Francisco Bay, you can see an island. It is very small but everybody knows its name – Alcatraz. Every year, more than 1.4 million visitors visit this place. And why do they all come? They want to learn more about the story of this terrible prison island.

Alcatraz Island first became an important prison in 1907 – at this time it was only a prison for soldiers. Then in the 1930s the US government needed a place for the most dangerous people in the country – people from wild cities like Chicago or New York. Soon they thought of Alcatraz Island. The water around the island is cold and dangerous to swim in – nobody could escape from there, the government thought.

Alcatraz Island

Al Capone

The island became a US government prison between 1934 and 1963, and over the years 1,545 men lived there. Alcatraz became the home of famous prisoners like Al Capone from Chicago and George 'Machine Gun' Kelly from Tennessee.

Life for the prisoners on Alcatraz was not easy. The island is only 2.4 kilometres away from the city of San Francisco. From their little dark rooms they could always hear the noises of city life from across the water. They were in prison and they could never forget it.

There are escape stories about thirty-six different men. Perhaps the most famous story is about Frank Morris and the two Anglin brothers, John and Clarence. At 9.30 on the evening of 11 June 1962 the three prisoners got into one of the building's big air vents with the help of spoons and other things from the prison. They carefully went through the air vents and out into the dark night.

The men took some old coats with them and made a raft – a type of little ship. Some time after ten o'clock they began to move across the fast, dangerous waters of San Francisco Bay on their raft.

And did the men escape? Some people think 'yes' but the prison said 'no' – the three prisoners died in the cold water, they said. But nobody found their dead bodies, only their raft, and nobody heard from them again.

You can learn all about their story in the exciting 1979 film *Escape from Alcatraz* with Clint Eastwood. Watch it and perhaps you can answer the question – did they escape or didn't they?

The prison closed in 1963. Later, in 1969, hundreds of Native Americans came to Alcatraz and stayed there for nineteen months. They were angry with the government about the terrible lives of their people. In the end, the government changed some of their ideas about Native Americans and they gave the people back some of their old villages and areas.

Alcatraz is now a US government park and you can visit the island all year. Most visitors come in the day but you can go at night too. Walk around the dark prison buildings, look in the rooms and listen for noises. Perhaps you can hear the prisoners from long ago . . .

A room in the prison

7   Golden Gate Park

Where do the people of San Francisco go when they want to escape city life? They walk or take the bus to the Golden Gate Park. You can find everything here – big fountains, tall trees, and of course beautiful gardens with flowers in every colour.

It is the biggest city park in the United States. It is 5 kilometres long and 1 kilometre across. And it is a very good place for runners and walkers, because you can go for more than 43 kilometres around the park.

The park began in the early 1870s when a famous man called William Hammond Hall and the Scottish gardener John McLaren started work on the area. They changed the place into a green garden. McLaren put in more than 155,000 trees and the park is famous for these today.

There are a lot of different parts of the park. For example, there is a beautiful Japanese garden. It was built by a man called Makoto Hagiwara in 1894 and it is the oldest Japanese garden in the United States. Visitors often come here and take photographs of the nice Japanese bridge.

The park has a lot of wonderful buildings too. The Conservatory of Flowers was built from wood and glass in 1878, and it has about 20,000 different flowers and little trees. You can find a lot of oranges and bananas in here too.

The Japanese Bridge

Buffalo

Skating in the park

When visitors walk through the park they sometimes see very big wild animals with long hair. But they do not need to feel afraid! These animals are the famous buffalo (American bison) and they first began to live here in 1894. They stay quietly in their area of the park and they cannot escape!

People in San Francisco love being out with their friends, and at the weekend everybody likes to play in the park. There are different places for tennis, football or baseball. You can see a lot of families and children on bicycles too.

The park is one of the best places for skaters – young students like to skate very fast here and sometimes jump wildly over things! Visitors often sit and watch – it is very exciting!

8 Going out

Going out in San Francisco is always interesting – you can watch the San Francisco Giants baseball team, see an exciting street parade, or visit one of the wonderful museums in the city.

One of the most famous museums is the Cable Car Museum. It is in a big old building in the Nob Hill neighbourhood. One of today's cable car lines finishes at the museum, and visitors can watch the big cables move here. There are a number of very old cable cars from the 1870s too.

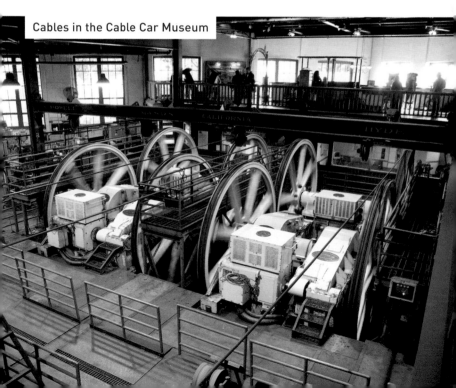

Cables in the Cable Car Museum

Schools often take children to the Wells Fargo Museum near the Chinatown neighbourhood. Here, students can learn all about the Wells Fargo stagecoaches from the early days of the gold rush.

Jump into an old stagecoach at the museum and you are on a wild road in the 1850s. Look into one of the famous Wells Fargo green boxes and what can you see? There are big bags of gold, old money, and letters from the time of the gold rush. Every stagecoach carried one of these boxes and the drivers always sat on them at the front.

A Wells Fargo green box

A new museum is the California Academy of Sciences in Golden Gate Park. The roof of the building is a wonderful colour because it has wild flowers all over it. When visitors walk through one part of the museum, they sometimes say, 'This is like South America!' That is because there are hundreds of trees and animals from places like the Amazon, and they are all alive!

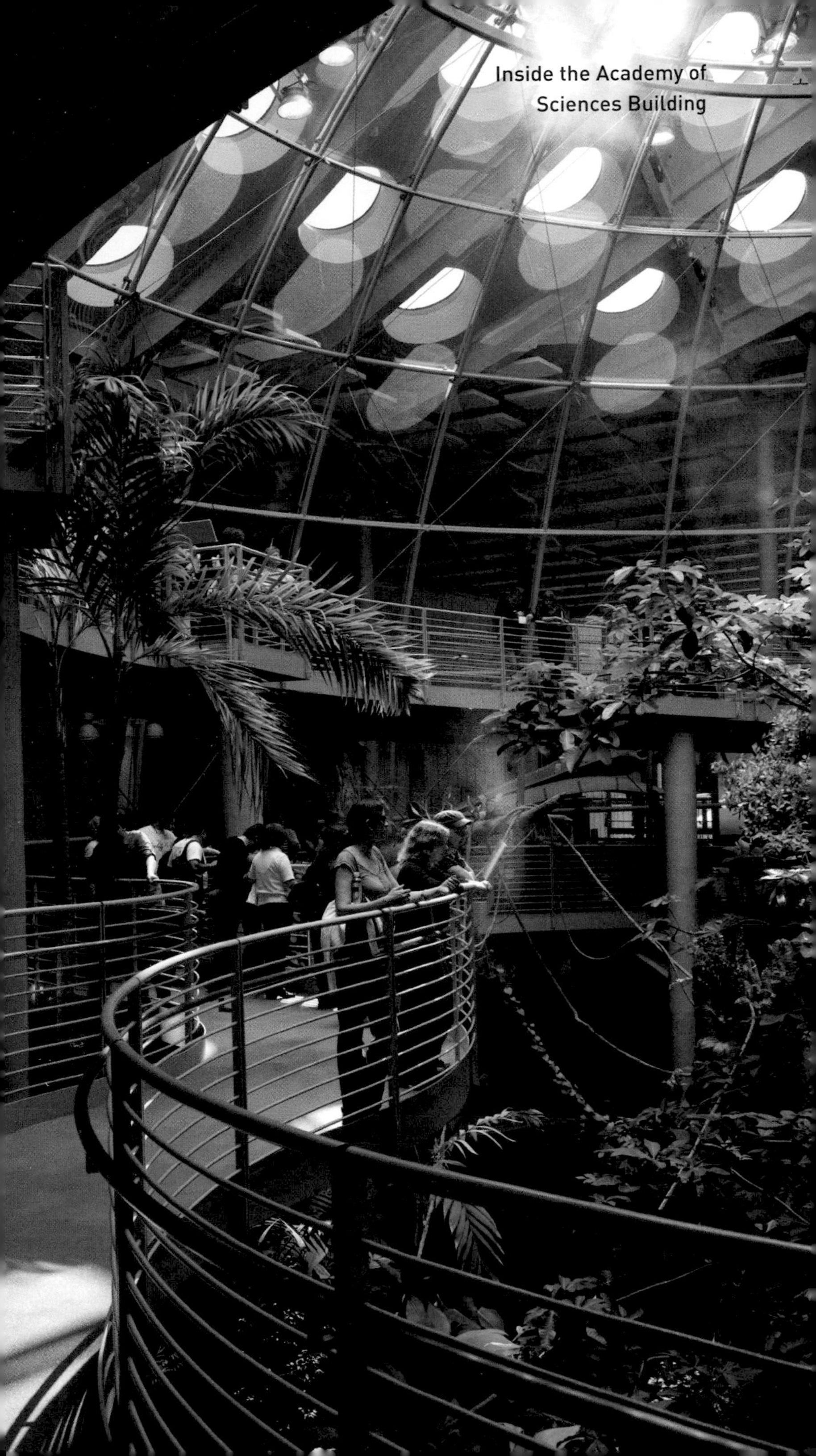

Inside the Academy of Sciences Building

Carrying the dragon in the New Year Parade

San Francisco is also famous for its big street parades. Every year in January or February there is the Chinese New Year parade. This began in 1858 and it is one of the biggest parades of its type. The best part is when a big gold dragon, 72 metres long, comes down the street. A hundred people walk along under the dragon and carry it from side to side through the streets of Chinatown.

On the Saturday before 17 March, there is the wonderful St Patrick's Day parade. The first parade was in 1852 and it is all about the best things from the country of Ireland. Thousands of people go down Market Street in the centre of the city. An important part of St Patrick's Day is the colour of people's clothes – everybody wears something green.

In their free time, a lot of people go to see the San Francisco 49ers American football team. The team takes its name from the men and women of the gold rush. What colours do they play in? Red and *gold*, of course! They were the first team in the important US Super Bowl five times in the 1980s and early 1990s.

The Giants are one of the oldest baseball teams in the United States. They began their life in New York but they moved to San Francisco in 1957. In 2010, they had a very good year when they won the famous World Series.

The team became very important on television in 1989 too. On 17 October, some minutes before the team began to play, the television pictures suddenly moved and then stopped. This was, of course, the Loma Prieta earthquake and it was the first earthquake 'on TV'.

Watching the San Francisco Giants

9 Shopping and eating

San Francisco is the home of many big shops like Bloomingdale's and Macy's. There is Neiman Marcus too – you can buy very expensive clothes here and nice things for your home. Visitors come and look at the beautiful roof in this building. It came from an old San Francisco shop called the City of Paris. The City of Paris opened in 1850 at the time of the gold rush. You could buy wonderful things from France here and people were sorry when it closed in 1972.

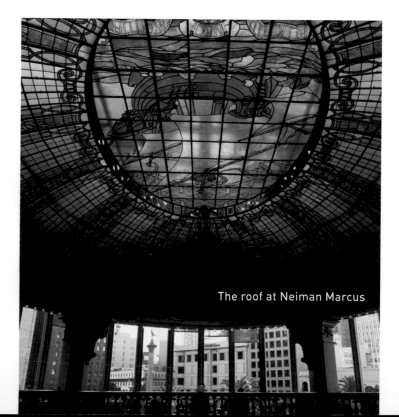
The roof at Neiman Marcus

The men and women of San Francisco love reading. They buy more books than the people of any other US city. The most famous bookshop is City Lights in the North Beach neighbourhood. A famous writer called Lawrence Ferlinghetti opened City Lights in 1953. It soon became an important centre for people with new ideas. People came from across the country to read the exciting books here by writers like Jack Kerouac.

City Lights is in a very interesting building too. It was built after the 1906 earthquake and it is a good example of an old San Francisco shop. You can walk past and look through the big old windows at the latest books.

After you finish shopping, you can go to one of the many restaurants. When people moved to San Francisco from China, Japan, South America, or Europe, they brought their ideas about food with them. So you can find good restaurants here from all over the world.

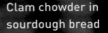
Clam chowder in sourdough bread

Perhaps some of the best places for food are the famous Boudin bread shops and restaurants. One of their biggest restaurants is at Fisherman's Wharf next to the water on San Francisco Bay. Visitors can look across to Alcatraz Island and the Golden Gate Bridge. Here you can eat some of the city's famous sourdough bread. Sourdough is a very old type of bread and many people love eating it.

At the time of the gold rush, sourdough bread was the most important food for people. They took it with them when they looked for gold in the hills. The Boudin family first began to make this bread in 1849 and you can learn all about their story in the Boudin museum.

People often ask for the most famous thing on the Boudin menu – clam chowder in sourdough bread. Clam chowder is made from seafood. You eat the warm chowder first with a spoon and then you finish the nice sourdough bread. When you are very hungry it is the best dinner in the world!

10   A little differently

San Francisco has a long and interesting story, from the early days of the gold rush to today. Some things about this city do not change – the white fog, the beautiful old houses, and the wonderful Golden Gate Bridge. But other things move with the times and of course, this city likes new ideas.

For example, the city recycles a lot of its old bottles, boxes, and newspapers. When you are walking around the city and you finish your drink, you can easily find a place for your old bottle. The city recycles 72 per cent of things like paper, old food, and bottles, and it is the best city in the United States for this.

Recycling in the city

The city also wants people to use 'greener' cars – these use electricity and they are not dirty like other cars. There are now a lot of places in the centre of San Francisco for people with these cars. They can put more electricity into them here and they do not need to pay for it. From May 2011 to December 2013, it is free.

With its newer ideas and wonderful older things like the world-famous cable cars or sourdough bread, we can look at the city and say 'San Francisco likes to do things a little differently'. And it is true, you cannot find a place like San Francisco in any other country in the world.

GLOSSARY

air vent an opening that lets air into a building
area a part of a town or country
around in many places in an area
bank a building or business for keeping money safely
become to grow or change and begin to be something
bus a kind of big 'car' which many people can travel in
business a place where people sell or make things
centre the part in the middle of something
chase *(n & v)* to run behind somebody and try to catch them
city a big and important town
coast the part of the land that is near the sea
dangerous something dangerous can hurt or kill you
disease an illness that you can catch from another person
earth the world; the ground under our feet
electricity power that comes through wires and makes machines work
escape to get free from somebody or something
film a story in pictures that you see at the cinema or on TV
fire the heat and bright light that comes from burning things
food what you eat
fountain a place where you can get a drink of water
government a group of people who control a country
idea a plan or new thought
internet the international network of computers that lets you see information from all over the world
island a piece of land with water around it
journey when you travel from one place to another
jump to move quickly off the ground, using your legs
life the time that you are alive; the way that you live
mission a building used by people who go to another country to teach people about Christianity
mountain a very high hill

museum   a place where you can look at old or interesting things
Native American   one of the people who were living in America before people came there from Europe
newspaper   large pieces of paper with news printed on them
other   different
park   a large place with trees and gardens where people can go to walk, play games etc.
part   one of the pieces of something
place   where something or somebody is
prison   a building for bad people; they stay there and cannot leave
railroad   trains and the tracks they move on
recycle   to do something to things like paper and glass so that they can be used again
restaurant   a place where people can buy and eat meals
side   the part of something that is not the top, bottom, front or back
soldier   a person in an army
spoon   a thing with a round end that you use for eating wet food
steep   a steep hill goes quickly from a low place to a high place
story   words that tell you about what happened in a certain place or time
streetcar   a kind of bus that uses electricity to move around a city
team   a group of people who play a sport together against another group
temperature   how hot or cold something is
terrible   very bad
travel   to go from one place to another place
type   a group of things that are the same in some way
use   to do a job with something
view   what you can see from a certain place
war   fighting between countries or groups of people
wild   without control; (of animals and flowers) living in nature, not with people
world   the earth with all its countries and people

San Francisco

ACTIVITIES

ACTIVITIES

Before Reading

1 Match the words to the pictures. You can use a dictionary.

1 ☐ bus   3 ☐ fire   5 ☐ mountain
2 ☐ coast   4 ☐ island   6 ☐ park

2 What do you know about San Francisco? Circle *a*, *b* or *c*.

1 You can visit an old prison. It's on _____.
   a) a mountain   b) an island   c) a ship

2 You can walk in the biggest _____ in an American city.
   a) park   b) museum   c) airport

3 You can see a very long _____. It's an orange-red colour.
   a) road   b) river   c) bridge

Do you know the names of these famous places? What do you know about them?

ACTIVITIES

While Reading

Read Chapter 1. Then fill in the gaps with these numbers.

3, 3, 4, 16, 43, 70, 1869, 1968, 800,000

1 _____ million people visit San Francisco every year.
2 The train journey takes _____ days from New York.
3 People first took the railroad across America in _____.
4 The city has water on _____ sides.
5 _____ men, women and children live in San Francisco.
6 There are _____ hills, and _____ of them have names.
7 There are _____ Chinese families in *The Joy Luck Club*.
8 The film with a long car chase is from the year _____.

Read Chapter 2. Put these events in the correct order.

1 The Ohlone went and worked at the mission but many died.
2 People heard about the gold rush and came to San Francisco.
3 The Ohlone lived quietly in the San Francisco area.
4 The Mexican town of Yerba Buena began.
5 The gold rush finished but many people stayed in the city.
6 James Marshall found gold in the river at Sutter's Mill.
7 A soldier came and made a building at the Golden Gate.
8 There was a war. After this, Yerba Buena became San Francisco.
9 Rich people built homes in places like Nob Hill.
10 The Spanish began their first mission at the Golden Gate.

Read Chapter 3, then rewrite these untrue sentences with the correct information.

1 The San Francisco earthquake was in the evening.
2 When the fires began people took water from the sea.
3 After the earthquake many people slept in the station.
4 In 1915 there was a small exhibition in San Francisco.
5 Aeroplanes were built in the city in the Second World War.
6 In the year 1967 people saw the 'Summer of Food' on TV.
7 San Francisco is famous for its new businesses and airports.

Read Chapters 4 and 5. Then match these halves of sentences.

1 The weather is often bad in . . .
2 The best weather is sometimes in . . .
3 The line of the San Andreas Fault goes near . . .
4 One of the most famous steep roads is . . .
5 You can find nice houses in different colours in . . .
6 The cable cars in the city began in . . .
7 The idea for the first cable car came from . . .
8 One famous streetcar conductor was . . .

a Lombard Street.
b June, July, and August.
c Maya Angelou.
d Alamo Square.
e April and May, or September and October.
f 1873.
g San Francisco to the south.
h Andrew Hallidie.

Read Chapter 6. Choose the best question-word for these questions, and then answer them.

How far / How many / How much / What / When / Who / Why

1 . . . had the first idea of a bridge at the Golden Gate?
2 . . . money did the Golden Gate Bridge cost?
3 . . . did the bridge first open?
4 . . . people walked across the bridge on the first day?
5 . . . happens on the bridge in the film *A View to a Kill*?
6 . . . people visit Alcatraz every year?
7 . . . is Alcatraz Island a good place for a prison?
8 . . . is Alcatraz from the city of San Francisco?
9 . . . prisoners escaped in June 1962?
10 . . . did Native Americans come to Alcatraz in 1969?

Read Chapter 7. Then circle *a*, *b* or *c*.

1 Golden Gate Park is bigger than any city park in _____.
   a) the world   b) Europe   c) the United States
2 You can run for more than ____ kilometres around the park.
   a) 5   b) 43   c) 187
3 John McLaren put a large number of ____ in the park.
   a) trees   b) bridges   c) buffalo
4 There is a famous _____ garden with a beautiful bridge.
   a) Scottish   b) American   c) Japanese
5 The buffalo first came to the park in the ____.
   a) 1870s   b) 1890s   c) 1920s
6 Golden Gate Park is a wonderful place for young _____.
   a) skaters   b) swimmers   c) shoppers

Read Chapters 8 and 9, then answer these questions.

1 Where is the Cable Car Museum? What can you find there?

2 What can you see in a green box at the Wells Fargo Museum?

3 What is different about the roof of the building at the Californian Academy of Sciences?

4 When did the famous Chinese New Year parade begin?

5 What colour do people wear on St Patrick's Day?

6 Why is the American football team called the 49ers?

7 What happened before the Giants played on 17 October 1989?

8 Where did the roof of the Neiman Marcus shop come from?

9 Why did people come to City Lights in the 1950s?

10 What can you see when you sit in the Boudin restaurant at Fisherman's Wharf?

11 When did the Boudin family first make sourdough bread?

12 What is clam chowder made from?

Read Chapter 10. Then circle the correct words.

1 People in San Francisco are interested in *new* / *old* ideas.

2 The city usually recycles things like *cars* / *newspapers*.

3 Finding a place for your old bottle is *easy* / *difficult*.

4 San Francisco is *worse* / *better* than other American cities for recycling.

5 The city wants drivers to have *greener* / *smaller* cars.

6 In the centre of the city people can easily put more *water* / *electricity* in their car.

7 People in San Francisco often do things *differently* / *quickly*.

ACTIVITIES

After Reading

1 Use the clues below to complete this crossword with words from this book. Then find the hidden ten-letter word.

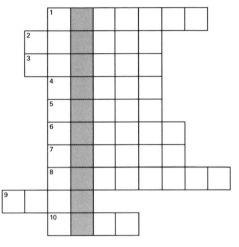

1 People in San Francisco usually _____ old bottles or boxes.

2 Visitors to the city often _____ around on cable cars.

3 In March there is always a big St Patrick's Day _____.

4 Lombard Street is on a very long _____ hill.

5 The film *Bullitt* is famous for a car _____ across the city.

6 There are green, blue, and yellow houses in Alamo _____.

7 In the Wells Fargo _____ you can find an old stagecoach.

8 From 1869 the _____ brought many people to the city.

9 Families often bring their bicycles to Golden Gate _____.

10 The San Francisco baseball _____ are called the Giants.

The hidden word in the crossword is _____.
Why does San Francisco have a lot of these?

2 Here are two postcards from different places in San Francisco. Complete them using the words below.

area / bigger / bridge / brothers / buffalo / building / dark / easy / escape / island / learned / Park / prison / prisoners / raft / stories / trees / visited

---

Hi there!

We're having a wonderful week in San Francisco. Yesterday, we went to a little _____ called Alcatraz. A long time ago there was a _____ here with very dangerous _____ like Al Capone.

We _____ all the different buildings on Alcatraz and we saw the prisoners' cold, _____ rooms. Life wasn't _____ here of course and a lot of the men wanted to _____!

We learned all about the different escape _____ on our visit. We were very interested in Frank Morris and the Anglin _____. They left the island one night in 1962. People later found their little _____ but they never saw the men again!

See you soon, Anna and Lucas

Hello!

I'm having a good time here in San Francisco. This morning I visited the famous Golden Gate _____ and I went for a very long walk. I _____ all about the place — it's _____ than any other city park in the United States!

I saw some very interesting things on my walk. I found a Japanese garden with a beautiful _____ and also a big _____ called the Conservatory of Flowers — it has about 20,000 flowers and little _____ in it. There are also some big _____ with long hair! But they don't walk around, they only live in one _____ of the park.

See you next week, Cara

Now write a postcard about a visit to the Golden Gate Bridge.

3 **Perhaps this is what some of the people in the book are thinking. Who are they? What is happening?**

1 'Why is she stopping under the bridge? I must stay close. But – oh no! She's jumping into the water! There's no time – I must jump in and get her. I'm coming, I'm coming . . .'

2 'What's that down there in the river? It looks like gold! That's exciting! I must talk to somebody about this. Perhaps John Sutter can help me.'

3 'I can't stay in this place any longer. This city isn't that far away – we just need to get across the water. And I've got an idea about that. I must talk to Clarence about it, and perhaps Frank too. San Francisco, here we come!'

4 **You are going to visit San Francisco for a weekend. Plan your visit. Think about these questions:**

• What time of year would you like to visit the city?
• What would you like to see and do there?
• Where would you like to stay?
• How would you like to travel about?
• What food would you like to eat?
• What places would you like to photograph?

ABOUT THE AUTHOR

Janet Hardy-Gould is an experienced teacher, writer, and teacher trainer. She is married with two children and lives in the ancient town of Lewes in the south of England. In her free time, she likes walking across the beautiful hills near her town and meeting friends in cafés for tea and cakes.

She has worked extensively on activities and support materials for OUP readers, notably for the Dominoes series and the Oxford Bookworms Library, and has published titles in both series. Her Bookworms titles are *King Arthur* (Human Interest), *Henry VIII and his Six Wives* (True Stories), *Deserts* (Factfiles), *Marco Polo and the Silk Road* (Factfiles), and *Chocolate* (Factfiles). For Dominoes she has written *The Great Fire of London*, *Mulan*, *Sinbad*, *The Travels of Ibn Battuta*, *Sherlock Holmes: The Emerald Crown*, *Hercules*, and *Ali Baba and the Forty Thieves*.

Janet loves travelling and has visited many different towns and cities in the United States. She first went to San Francisco on a Greyhound bus in 1987 and has been fascinated by the city ever since. Over the years she has particularly enjoyed watching the many films set in the rolling hills of San Francisco. Her favourite film is Alfred Hitchcock's *Vertigo* with its famous scene under Golden Gate Bridge.

OXFORD BOOKWORMS LIBRARY

*Classics • Crime & Mystery • Factfiles • Fantasy & Horror
Human Interest • Playscripts • Thriller & Adventure
True Stories • World Stories*

The OXFORD BOOKWORMS LIBRARY provides enjoyable reading in English, with a wide range of classic and modern fiction, non-fiction, and plays. It includes original and adapted texts in seven carefully graded language stages, which take learners from beginner to advanced level. An overview is given on the next pages.

All Stage 1 titles are available as audio recordings, as well as over eighty other titles from Starter to Stage 6. All Starters and many titles at Stages 1 to 4 are specially recommended for younger learners. Every Bookworm is illustrated, and Starters and Factfiles have full-colour illustrations.

The OXFORD BOOKWORMS LIBRARY also offers extensive support. Each book contains an introduction to the story, notes about the author, a glossary, and activities. Additional resources include tests and worksheets, and answers for these and for the activities in the books. There is advice on running a class library, using audio recordings, and the many ways of using Oxford Bookworms in reading programmes. Resource materials are available on the website <www.oup.com/bookworms>.

The *Oxford Bookworms Collection* is a series for advanced learners. It consists of volumes of short stories by well-known authors, both classic and modern. Texts are not abridged or adapted in any way, but carefully selected to be accessible to the advanced student.

You can find details and a full list of titles in the *Oxford Bookworms Library Catalogue* and *Oxford English Language Teaching Catalogues*, and on the website <www.oup.com/bookworms>.

THE OXFORD BOOKWORMS LIBRARY
GRADING AND SAMPLE EXTRACTS

STARTER • 250 HEADWORDS

present simple – present continuous – imperative –
can/cannot, must – *going to* (future) – simple gerunds ...

Her phone is ringing – but where is it?

Sally gets out of bed and looks in her bag. No phone.
She looks under the bed. No phone. Then she looks behind
the door. There is her phone. Sally picks up her phone and
answers it. *Sally's Phone*

STAGE 1 • 400 HEADWORDS

... past simple – coordination with *and*, *but*, *or* –
subordination with *before*, *after*, *when*, *because*, *so* ...

I knew him in Persia. He was a famous builder and I
worked with him there. For a time I was his friend, but
not for long. When he came to Paris, I came after him –
I wanted to watch him. He was a very clever, very
dangerous man. *The Phantom of the Opera*

STAGE 2 • 700 HEADWORDS

... present perfect – *will* (future) – *(don't) have to, must not, could* –
comparison of adjectives – simple *if* clauses – past continuous –
tag questions – *ask/tell* + infinitive ...

While I was writing these words in my diary, I decided
what to do. I must try to escape. I shall try to get down the
wall outside. The window is high above the ground, but
I have to try. I shall take some of the gold with me – if I
escape, perhaps it will be helpful later. *Dracula*

STAGE 3 • 1000 HEADWORDS

... *should, may* – present perfect continuous – *used to* – past perfect –
causative – relative clauses – indirect statements ...

Of course, it was most important that no one should see
Colin, Mary, or Dickon entering the secret garden. So Colin
gave orders to the gardeners that they must all keep away
from that part of the garden in future. *The Secret Garden*

STAGE 4 • 1400 HEADWORDS

... past perfect continuous – passive (simple forms) –
would conditional clauses – indirect questions –
relatives with *where/when* – gerunds after prepositions/phrases ...

I was glad. Now Hyde could not show his face to the world
again. If he did, every honest man in London would be proud
to report him to the police. *Dr Jekyll and Mr Hyde*

STAGE 5 • 1800 HEADWORDS

... future continuous – future perfect –
passive (modals, continuous forms) –
would have conditional clauses – modals + perfect infinitive ...

If he had spoken Estella's name, I would have hit him. I was so
angry with him, and so depressed about my future, that I could
not eat the breakfast. Instead I went straight to the old house.
Great Expectations

STAGE 6 • 2500 HEADWORDS

... passive (infinitives, gerunds) – advanced modal meanings –
clauses of concession, condition

When I stepped up to the piano, I was confident. It was as if I
knew that the prodigy side of me really did exist. And when I
started to play, I was so caught up in how lovely I looked that
I didn't worry how I would sound. *The Joy Luck Club*

BOOKWORMS · FACTFILES · STAGE 1

New York

JOHN ESCOTT

What can you do in New York? Everything! You can go to some of the world's most famous shops, watch a baseball game, go to the top of a skyscraper, see a concert in Central Park, eat a sandwich in a New York deli, see a show in a Broadway theatre.

New York is big, noisy, and exciting, and it's waiting for you. Open the book and come with us to this wonderful city.

BOOKWORMS · FACTFILES · STAGE 2

Marco Polo and the Silk Road

JANET HARDY-GOULD

For a child in the great city of Venice in the thirteenth century, there could be nothing better than the stories of sailors. There were stories of strange animals, wonderful cities, sweet spices, and terrible wild deserts where a traveller could die. One young boy listened, waited, and dreamed. Perhaps one day his father and uncle would return. Perhaps he too could travel with them to great markets in faraway places. For young Marco Polo, later the greatest traveller of his time, a dangerous, exciting world was waiting . . .